This notebook belongs to:

_____

Published by: Character Designs

PROJECT NAME: _____ DATE: _____

NOTES	BRAINSTORMING

Timeline	Step 1.	Step 2.	Step 3.	Step 4.
Pain point				
Touchpoint				
Channel				
Experience				

PROJECT NAME: _____ DATE: _____

NOTES	BRAINSTORMING

Timeline	Step 1.	Step 2.	Step 3.	Step 4.
Pain point				
Touchpoint				
Channel				
Experience				

PROJECT NAME: _____   DATE: _____

NOTES	BRAINSTORMING

Timeline	Step 1.	Step 2.	Step 3.	Step 4.
Pain point				
Touchpoint				
Channel				
Experience				

PROJECT NAME: _____   DATE: _____

NOTES	BRAINSTORMING

Timeline	Step 1.	Step 2.	Step 3.	Step 4.
Pain point				
Touchpoint				
Channel				
Experience				

PROJECT NAME: _____   DATE: _____

NOTES	BRAINSTORMING

Timeline	Step 1.	Step 2.	Step 3.	Step 4.
Pain point				
Touchpoint				
Channel				
Experience				

PROJECT NAME: _____   DATE: _____

NOTES	BRAINSTORMING

Timeline	Step 1.	Step 2.	Step 3.	Step 4.
Pain point				
Touchpoint				
Channel				
Experience				

PROJECT NAME: _____   DATE: _____

NOTES	BRAINSTORMING

Timeline	Step 1.	Step 2.	Step 3.	Step 4.
Pain point				
Touchpoint				
Channel				
Experience				

PROJECT NAME: _____   DATE: _____

NOTES	BRAINSTORMING

Timeline	Step 1.	Step 2.	Step 3.	Step 4.
Pain point				
Touchpoint				
Channel				
Experience				

PROJECT NAME: _____   DATE: _____

NOTES	BRAINSTORMING

Timeline	Step 1.	Step 2.	Step 3.	Step 4.
Pain point				
Touchpoint				
Channel				
Experience				

PROJECT NAME: _____   DATE: _____

NOTES	BRAINSTORMING

Timeline	Step 1.	Step 2.	Step 3.	Step 4.
Pain point				
Touchpoint				
Channel				
Experience				

PROJECT NAME: _____   DATE: _____

NOTES	BRAINSTORMING

Timeline	Step 1.	Step 2.	Step 3.	Step 4.
Pain point				
Touchpoint				
Channel				
Experience				

PROJECT NAME: _____   DATE: _____

NOTES	BRAINSTORMING

Timeline	Step 1.	Step 2.	Step 3.	Step 4.
Pain point				
Touchpoint				
Channel				
Experience				

PROJECT NAME: _____   DATE: _____

NOTES	BRAINSTORMING

Timeline	Step 1.	Step 2.	Step 3.	Step 4.
Pain point				
Touchpoint				
Channel				
Experience				

PROJECT NAME: _____   DATE: _____

NOTES	BRAINSTORMING

Timeline	Step 1.	Step 2.	Step 3.	Step 4.
Pain point				
Touchpoint				
Channel				
Experience				

PROJECT NAME: _____   DATE: _____

NOTES	BRAINSTORMING

Timeline	Step 1.	Step 2.	Step 3.	Step 4.
Pain point				
Touchpoint				
Channel				
Experience				

PROJECT NAME: _____   DATE: _____

NOTES	BRAINSTORMING

Timeline	Step 1.	Step 2.	Step 3.	Step 4.
Pain point				
Touchpoint				
Channel				
Experience				

PROJECT NAME: _____   DATE: _____

NOTES	BRAINSTORMING

Timeline	Step 1.	Step 2.	Step 3.	Step 4.
Pain point				
Touchpoint				
Channel				
Experience				

PROJECT NAME: _____   DATE: _____

NOTES	BRAINSTORMING

Timeline	Step 1.	Step 2.	Step 3.	Step 4.
Pain point				
Touchpoint				
Channel				
Experience				

PROJECT NAME: _____   DATE: _____

NOTES	BRAINSTORMING

Timeline	Step 1.	Step 2.	Step 3.	Step 4.
Pain point				
Touchpoint				
Channel				
Experience				

PROJECT NAME: _____   DATE: _____

NOTES	BRAINSTORMING

Timeline	Step 1.	Step 2.	Step 3.	Step 4.
Pain point				
Touchpoint				
Channel				
Experience				

PROJECT NAME: _____   DATE: _____

NOTES	BRAINSTORMING

Timeline	Step 1.	Step 2.	Step 3.	Step 4.
Pain point				
Touchpoint				
Channel				
Experience				

PROJECT NAME: _____   DATE: _____

NOTES	BRAINSTORMING

Timeline	Step 1.	Step 2.	Step 3.	Step 4.
Pain point				
Touchpoint				
Channel				
Experience				

PROJECT NAME: _____   DATE: _____

NOTES	BRAINSTORMING

Timeline	Step 1.	Step 2.	Step 3.	Step 4.
Pain point				
Touchpoint				
Channel				
Experience				

PROJECT NAME: _____   DATE: _____

NOTES	BRAINSTORMING

Timeline	Step 1.	Step 2.	Step 3.	Step 4.
Pain point				
Touchpoint				
Channel				
Experience				

PROJECT NAME: _____   DATE: _____

NOTES	BRAINSTORMING

Timeline	Step 1.	Step 2.	Step 3.	Step 4.
Pain point				
Touchpoint				
Channel				
Experience				

PROJECT NAME: _____   DATE: _____

NOTES	BRAINSTORMING

Timeline	Step 1.	Step 2.	Step 3.	Step 4.
Pain point				
Touchpoint				
Channel				
Experience				

PROJECT NAME: _____   DATE: _____

NOTES	BRAINSTORMING

Timeline	Step 1.	Step 2.	Step 3.	Step 4.
Pain point				
Touchpoint				
Channel				
Experience				

PROJECT NAME: _____   DATE: _____

NOTES	BRAINSTORMING

Timeline	Step 1.	Step 2.	Step 3.	Step 4.
Pain point				
Touchpoint				
Channel				
Experience				

PROJECT NAME: _____   DATE: _____

NOTES	BRAINSTORMING

Timeline	Step 1.	Step 2.	Step 3.	Step 4.
Pain point				
Touchpoint				
Channel				
Experience				

PROJECT NAME: _____   DATE: _____

NOTES	BRAINSTORMING

Timeline	Step 1.	Step 2.	Step 3.	Step 4.
Pain point				
Touchpoint				
Channel				
Experience				

PROJECT NAME: _____   DATE: _____

NOTES	BRAINSTORMING

Timeline	Step 1.	Step 2.	Step 3.	Step 4.
Pain point				
Touchpoint				
Channel				
Experience				

PROJECT NAME: _____   DATE: _____

NOTES	BRAINSTORMING

Timeline	Step 1.	Step 2.	Step 3.	Step 4.
Pain point				
Touchpoint				
Channel				
Experience				

PROJECT NAME: _____   DATE: _____

NOTES	BRAINSTORMING

Timeline	Step 1.	Step 2.	Step 3.	Step 4.
Pain point				
Touchpoint				
Channel				
Experience				

PROJECT NAME: _____   DATE: _____

NOTES	BRAINSTORMING

Timeline	Step 1.	Step 2.	Step 3.	Step 4.
Pain point				
Touchpoint				
Channel				
Experience				

PROJECT NAME: _____   DATE: _____

NOTES	BRAINSTORMING

Timeline	Step 1.	Step 2.	Step 3.	Step 4.
Pain point				
Touchpoint				
Channel				
Experience				

PROJECT NAME: _____   DATE: _____

NOTES	BRAINSTORMING

Timeline	Step 1.	Step 2.	Step 3.	Step 4.
Pain point				
Touchpoint				
Channel				
Experience				

PROJECT NAME: _____ DATE: _____

NOTES	BRAINSTORMING

Timeline	Step 1.	Step 2.	Step 3.	Step 4.
Pain point				
Touchpoint				
Channel				
Experience				

PROJECT NAME: _____   DATE: _____

NOTES	BRAINSTORMING

Timeline	Step 1.	Step 2.	Step 3.	Step 4.
Pain point				
Touchpoint				
Channel				
Experience				

PROJECT NAME: _____   DATE: _____

NOTES	BRAINSTORMING

Timeline	Step 1.	Step 2.	Step 3.	Step 4.
Pain point				
Touchpoint				
Channel				
Experience				

PROJECT NAME: _____   DATE: _____

NOTES	BRAINSTORMING

Timeline	Step 1.	Step 2.	Step 3.	Step 4.
Pain point				
Touchpoint				
Channel				
Experience				

PROJECT NAME: _____   DATE: _____

NOTES	BRAINSTORMING

Timeline	Step 1.	Step 2.	Step 3.	Step 4.
Pain point				
Touchpoint				
Channel				
Experience				

PROJECT NAME: _____   DATE: _____

NOTES	BRAINSTORMING

Timeline	Step 1.	Step 2.	Step 3.	Step 4.
Pain point				
Touchpoint				
Channel				
Experience				

PROJECT NAME: _____   DATE: _____

NOTES	BRAINSTORMING

Timeline	Step 1.	Step 2.	Step 3.	Step 4.
Pain point				
Touchpoint				
Channel				
Experience				

PROJECT NAME: _____   DATE: _____

NOTES	BRAINSTORMING

Timeline	Step 1.	Step 2.	Step 3.	Step 4.
Pain point				
Touchpoint				
Channel				
Experience				

PROJECT NAME: _____   DATE: _____

NOTES	BRAINSTORMING

Timeline	Step 1.	Step 2.	Step 3.	Step 4.
Pain point				
Touchpoint				
Channel				
Experience				

PROJECT NAME: _____   DATE: _____

NOTES	BRAINSTORMING

Timeline	Step 1.	Step 2.	Step 3.	Step 4.
Pain point				
Touchpoint				
Channel				
Experience				

PROJECT NAME: _____   DATE: _____

NOTES	BRAINSTORMING

Timeline	Step 1.	Step 2.	Step 3.	Step 4.
Pain point				
Touchpoint				
Channel				
Experience				

PROJECT NAME: _____   DATE: _____

NOTES	BRAINSTORMING

Timeline	Step 1.	Step 2.	Step 3.	Step 4.
Pain point				
Touchpoint				
Channel				
Experience				

PROJECT NAME: _____   DATE: _____

NOTES	BRAINSTORMING

Timeline	Step 1.	Step 2.	Step 3.	Step 4.
Pain point				
Touchpoint				
Channel				
Experience				

PROJECT NAME: _____   DATE: _____

NOTES	BRAINSTORMING

Timeline	Step 1.	Step 2.	Step 3.	Step 4.
Pain point				
Touchpoint				
Channel				
Experience				

PROJECT NAME: _____   DATE: _____

NOTES	BRAINSTORMING

Timeline	Step 1.	Step 2.	Step 3.	Step 4.
Pain point				
Touchpoint				
Channel				
Experience				

PROJECT NAME: _____   DATE: _____

NOTES	BRAINSTORMING

Timeline	Step 1.	Step 2.	Step 3.	Step 4.
Pain point				
Touchpoint				
Channel				
Experience				

PROJECT NAME: _____   DATE: _____

NOTES	BRAINSTORMING

Timeline	Step 1.	Step 2.	Step 3.	Step 4.
Pain point				
Touchpoint				
Channel				
Experience				

PROJECT NAME: _____   DATE: _____

NOTES	BRAINSTORMING

Timeline	Step 1.	Step 2.	Step 3.	Step 4.
Pain point				
Touchpoint				
Channel				
Experience				

PROJECT NAME: _____   DATE: _____

NOTES	BRAINSTORMING

Timeline	Step 1.	Step 2.	Step 3.	Step 4.
Pain point				
Touchpoint				
Channel				
Experience				

PROJECT NAME: _____   DATE: _____

NOTES	BRAINSTORMING

Timeline	Step 1.	Step 2.	Step 3.	Step 4.
Pain point				
Touchpoint				
Channel				
Experience				

PROJECT NAME: _____   DATE: _____

NOTES	BRAINSTORMING

Timeline	Step 1.	Step 2.	Step 3.	Step 4.
Pain point				
Touchpoint				
Channel				
Experience				

PROJECT NAME: _____   DATE: _____

NOTES	BRAINSTORMING

Timeline	Step 1.	Step 2.	Step 3.	Step 4.
Pain point				
Touchpoint				
Channel				
Experience				

PROJECT NAME: _____ DATE: _____

NOTES	BRAINSTORMING

Timeline	Step 1.	Step 2.	Step 3.	Step 4.
Pain point				
Touchpoint				
Channel				
Experience				

PROJECT NAME: _____   DATE: _____

NOTES	BRAINSTORMING

Timeline	Step 1.	Step 2.	Step 3.	Step 4.
Pain point				
Touchpoint				
Channel				
Experience				

PROJECT NAME: _____   DATE: _____

NOTES	BRAINSTORMING

Timeline	Step 1.	Step 2.	Step 3.	Step 4.
Pain point				
Touchpoint				
Channel				
Experience				

PROJECT NAME: _____   DATE: _____

NOTES	BRAINSTORMING

Timeline	Step 1.	Step 2.	Step 3.	Step 4.
Pain point				
Touchpoint				
Channel				
Experience				

PROJECT NAME: _____   DATE: _____

NOTES	BRAINSTORMING

Timeline	Step 1.	Step 2.	Step 3.	Step 4.
Pain point				
Touchpoint				
Channel				
Experience				

PROJECT NAME: _____   DATE: _____

NOTES	BRAINSTORMING

Timeline	Step 1.	Step 2.	Step 3.	Step 4.
Pain point				
Touchpoint				
Channel				
Experience				

PROJECT NAME: _____   DATE: _____

NOTES	BRAINSTORMING

Timeline	Step 1.	Step 2.	Step 3.	Step 4.
Pain point				
Touchpoint				
Channel				
Experience				

PROJECT NAME: _____   DATE: _____

NOTES	BRAINSTORMING

Timeline	Step 1.	Step 2.	Step 3.	Step 4.
Pain point				
Touchpoint				
Channel				
Experience				

PROJECT NAME: _____   DATE: _____

NOTES	BRAINSTORMING

Timeline	Step 1.	Step 2.	Step 3.	Step 4.
Pain point				
Touchpoint				
Channel				
Experience				

PROJECT NAME: _____   DATE: _____

NOTES	BRAINSTORMING

Timeline	Step 1.	Step 2.	Step 3.	Step 4.
Pain point				
Touchpoint				
Channel				
Experience				

PROJECT NAME: _____   DATE: _____

NOTES	BRAINSTORMING

Timeline	Step 1.	Step 2.	Step 3.	Step 4.
Pain point				
Touchpoint				
Channel				
Experience				

PROJECT NAME: _____   DATE: _____

NOTES	BRAINSTORMING

Timeline	Step 1.	Step 2.	Step 3.	Step 4.
Pain point				
Touchpoint				
Channel				
Experience				

PROJECT NAME: _____   DATE: _____

NOTES	BRAINSTORMING

Timeline	Step 1.	Step 2.	Step 3.	Step 4.
Pain point				
Touchpoint				
Channel				
Experience				

PROJECT NAME: _____   DATE: _____

NOTES	BRAINSTORMING

Timeline	Step 1.	Step 2.	Step 3.	Step 4.
Pain point				
Touchpoint				
Channel				
Experience				

PROJECT NAME: _____   DATE: _____

NOTES	BRAINSTORMING

Timeline	Step 1.	Step 2.	Step 3.	Step 4.
Pain point				
Touchpoint				
Channel				
Experience				

PROJECT NAME: _____   DATE: _____

NOTES	BRAINSTORMING

Timeline	Step 1.	Step 2.	Step 3.	Step 4.
Pain point				
Touchpoint				
Channel				
Experience				

PROJECT NAME: _____   DATE: _____

NOTES	BRAINSTORMING

Timeline	Step 1.	Step 2.	Step 3.	Step 4.
Pain point				
Touchpoint				
Channel				
Experience				

PROJECT NAME: _____   DATE: _____

NOTES	BRAINSTORMING

Timeline	Step 1.	Step 2.	Step 3.	Step 4.
Pain point				
Touchpoint				
Channel				
Experience				

PROJECT NAME: _____   DATE: _____

NOTES	BRAINSTORMING

Timeline	Step 1.	Step 2.	Step 3.	Step 4.
Pain point				
Touchpoint				
Channel				
Experience				

PROJECT NAME: _____ DATE: _____

NOTES	BRAINSTORMING

Timeline	Step 1.	Step 2.	Step 3.	Step 4.
Pain point				
Touchpoint				
Channel				
Experience				

PROJECT NAME: _____   DATE: _____

NOTES	BRAINSTORMING

Timeline	Step 1.	Step 2.	Step 3.	Step 4.
Pain point				
Touchpoint				
Channel				
Experience				

PROJECT NAME: _____   DATE: _____

NOTES	BRAINSTORMING

Timeline	Step 1.	Step 2.	Step 3.	Step 4.
Pain point				
Touchpoint				
Channel				
Experience				

PROJECT NAME: _____   DATE: _____

NOTES	BRAINSTORMING

Timeline	Step 1.	Step 2.	Step 3.	Step 4.
Pain point				
Touchpoint				
Channel				
Experience				

PROJECT NAME: _____   DATE: _____

NOTES	BRAINSTORMING

Timeline	Step 1.	Step 2.	Step 3.	Step 4.
Pain point				
Touchpoint				
Channel				
Experience				

PROJECT NAME: _____   DATE: _____

NOTES	BRAINSTORMING

Timeline	Step 1.	Step 2.	Step 3.	Step 4.
Pain point				
Touchpoint				
Channel				
Experience				

PROJECT NAME: _____   DATE: _____

NOTES	BRAINSTORMING

Timeline	Step 1.	Step 2.	Step 3.	Step 4.
Pain point				
Touchpoint				
Channel				
Experience				

PROJECT NAME: _____   DATE: _____

NOTES	BRAINSTORMING

Timeline	Step 1.	Step 2.	Step 3.	Step 4.
Pain point				
Touchpoint				
Channel				
Experience				

PROJECT NAME: _____   DATE: _____

NOTES	BRAINSTORMING

Timeline	Step 1.	Step 2.	Step 3.	Step 4.
Pain point				
Touchpoint				
Channel				
Experience				

PROJECT NAME: _____   DATE: _____

NOTES	BRAINSTORMING

Timeline	Step 1.	Step 2.	Step 3.	Step 4.
Pain point				
Touchpoint				
Channel				
Experience				

PROJECT NAME: _____   DATE: _____

NOTES	BRAINSTORMING

Timeline	Step 1.	Step 2.	Step 3.	Step 4.
Pain point				
Touchpoint				
Channel				
Experience				

PROJECT NAME: _____   DATE: _____

NOTES	BRAINSTORMING

Timeline	Step 1.	Step 2.	Step 3.	Step 4.
Pain point				
Touchpoint				
Channel				
Experience				

PROJECT NAME: _____   DATE: _____

NOTES	BRAINSTORMING

Timeline	Step 1.	Step 2.	Step 3.	Step 4.
Pain point				
Touchpoint				
Channel				
Experience				

PROJECT NAME: _____   DATE: _____

NOTES	BRAINSTORMING

Timeline	Step 1.	Step 2.	Step 3.	Step 4.
Pain point				
Touchpoint				
Channel				
Experience				

PROJECT NAME: _____   DATE: _____

NOTES	BRAINSTORMING

Timeline	Step 1.	Step 2.	Step 3.	Step 4.
Pain point				
Touchpoint				
Channel				
Experience				

PROJECT NAME: _____   DATE: _____

NOTES	BRAINSTORMING

Timeline	Step 1.	Step 2.	Step 3.	Step 4.
Pain point				
Touchpoint				
Channel				
Experience				

PROJECT NAME: _____   DATE: _____

NOTES	BRAINSTORMING

Timeline	Step 1.	Step 2.	Step 3.	Step 4.
Pain point				
Touchpoint				
Channel				
Experience				

PROJECT NAME: _____   DATE: _____

NOTES	BRAINSTORMING

Timeline	Step 1.	Step 2.	Step 3.	Step 4.
Pain point				
Touchpoint				
Channel				
Experience				

PROJECT NAME: _____   DATE: _____

NOTES	BRAINSTORMING

Timeline	Step 1.	Step 2.	Step 3.	Step 4.
Pain point				
Touchpoint				
Channel				
Experience				

PROJECT NAME: _____   DATE: _____

NOTES	BRAINSTORMING

Timeline	Step 1.	Step 2.	Step 3.	Step 4.
Pain point				
Touchpoint				
Channel				
Experience				

PROJECT NAME: _____   DATE: _____

NOTES	BRAINSTORMING

Timeline	Step 1.	Step 2.	Step 3.	Step 4.
Pain point				
Touchpoint				
Channel				
Experience				

PROJECT NAME: _____   DATE: _____

NOTES	BRAINSTORMING

Timeline	Step 1.	Step 2.	Step 3.	Step 4.
Pain point				
Touchpoint				
Channel				
Experience				

PROJECT NAME: _____   DATE: _____

NOTES	BRAINSTORMING

Timeline	Step 1.	Step 2.	Step 3.	Step 4.
Pain point				
Touchpoint				
Channel				
Experience				

PROJECT NAME: _____   DATE: _____

NOTES	BRAINSTORMING

Timeline	Step 1.	Step 2.	Step 3.	Step 4.
Pain point				
Touchpoint				
Channel				
Experience				

PROJECT NAME: _____   DATE: _____

NOTES	BRAINSTORMING

Timeline	Step 1.	Step 2.	Step 3.	Step 4.
Pain point				
Touchpoint				
Channel				
Experience				

PROJECT NAME: _____   DATE: _____

NOTES	BRAINSTORMING

Timeline	Step 1.	Step 2.	Step 3.	Step 4.
Pain point				
Touchpoint				
Channel				
Experience				

PROJECT NAME: _____   DATE: _____

NOTES	BRAINSTORMING

Timeline	Step 1.	Step 2.	Step 3.	Step 4.
Pain point				
Touchpoint				
Channel				
Experience				

PROJECT NAME: _____ DATE: _____

NOTES	BRAINSTORMING

Timeline	Step 1.	Step 2.	Step 3.	Step 4.
Pain point				
Touchpoint				
Channel				
Experience				

PROJECT NAME: _____   DATE: _____

NOTES	BRAINSTORMING

Timeline	Step 1.	Step 2.	Step 3.	Step 4.
Pain point				
Touchpoint				
Channel				
Experience				

PROJECT NAME: _____   DATE: _____

NOTES	BRAINSTORMING

Timeline	Step 1.	Step 2.	Step 3.	Step 4.
Pain point				
Touchpoint				
Channel				
Experience				

PROJECT NAME: _____   DATE: _____

NOTES	BRAINSTORMING

Timeline	Step 1.	Step 2.	Step 3.	Step 4.
Pain point				
Touchpoint				
Channel				
Experience				

PROJECT NAME: _____   DATE: _____

NOTES	BRAINSTORMING

Timeline	Step 1.	Step 2.	Step 3.	Step 4.
Pain point				
Touchpoint				
Channel				
Experience				

PROJECT NAME: _____   DATE: _____

NOTES	BRAINSTORMING

Timeline	Step 1.	Step 2.	Step 3.	Step 4.
Pain point				
Touchpoint				
Channel				
Experience				

PROJECT NAME: _____   DATE: _____

NOTES	BRAINSTORMING

Timeline	Step 1.	Step 2.	Step 3.	Step 4.
Pain point				
Touchpoint				
Channel				
Experience				

PROJECT NAME: _____   DATE: _____

NOTES	BRAINSTORMING

Timeline	Step 1.	Step 2.	Step 3.	Step 4.
Pain point				
Touchpoint				
Channel				
Experience				

PROJECT NAME: _____   DATE: _____

NOTES	BRAINSTORMING

Timeline	Step 1.	Step 2.	Step 3.	Step 4.
Pain point				
Touchpoint				
Channel				
Experience				

PROJECT NAME: _____   DATE: _____

NOTES	BRAINSTORMING

Timeline	Step 1.	Step 2.	Step 3.	Step 4.
Pain point				
Touchpoint				
Channel				
Experience				

PROJECT NAME: _____   DATE: _____

NOTES	BRAINSTORMING

Timeline	Step 1.	Step 2.	Step 3.	Step 4.
Pain point				
Touchpoint				
Channel				
Experience				

PROJECT NAME: _____   DATE: _____

NOTES	BRAINSTORMING

Timeline	Step 1.	Step 2.	Step 3.	Step 4.
Pain point				
Touchpoint				
Channel				
Experience				

PROJECT NAME: _____   DATE: _____

NOTES	BRAINSTORMING

Timeline	Step 1.	Step 2.	Step 3.	Step 4.
Pain point				
Touchpoint				
Channel				
Experience				

PROJECT NAME: _____   DATE: _____

NOTES	BRAINSTORMING

Timeline	Step 1.	Step 2.	Step 3.	Step 4.
Pain point				
Touchpoint				
Channel				
Experience				

PROJECT NAME: _____   DATE: _____

NOTES	BRAINSTORMING

Timeline	Step 1.	Step 2.	Step 3.	Step 4.
Pain point				
Touchpoint				
Channel				
Experience				

PROJECT NAME: _____   DATE: _____

NOTES	BRAINSTORMING

Timeline	Step 1.	Step 2.	Step 3.	Step 4.
Pain point				
Touchpoint				
Channel				
Experience				

Takeaway notes:

_____

_____

_____

_____

_____

Year of use:

_____